Margaret Strider

Margaret Strider

Designs for Theatre

DESIGNS FOR

Hood Museum of Art

THEATRE

In association with the

STRATFORD

Stratford Shakespearean Festival Foundation

FESTIVAL

of Canada

1954–1990

LIBRARY OF CONGRESS CATALOGING-IN-PUBLICATION DATA

Hood Museum of Art.
Stratford Festival costume designs, 1954–1990.
p.   cm.
ISBN 0-944722-06-7
1. Stratford Festival (Ont.)—Exhibitions.   2. Costume—
Exhibitions.   I. Title.
PN2306. S77H66   1990
792′.026′07471323—dc20
90-48680
CIP

REPRODUCTION CREDITS
Jeffrey Nintzel, cat. nos. 4, 17, 25, 32;
all other drawings were scanned from originals.

This catalogue was published in conjunction with an exhibition organized to
celebrate the residency of the Stratford Festival at the Hopkins Center, Dartmouth College, November 12–18, 1990. The exhibition was shown in the
Harrington Gallery of the Hood Museum of Art from
November 9, 1990 to January 13, 1991.

All drawings are lent courtesy of the Stratford Festival Archives,
Stratford Shakespearean Festival Foundation of Canada,
Stratford, Ontario

Printed and bound by Meriden-Stinehour Press
Designed by Christopher Kuntze

CONTENTS

PREFACE

*M*arking the occasion of the Stratford Festival company's residency at Dartmouth College in November 1990, this book has been conceived to accompany and document an exhibition of drawings selected from the Archives of the Stratford Festival in Stratford, Ontario.

We are grateful to James Cuno, Director of the Hood Museum of Art at Dartmouth College, for developing the concept of this exhibition and for selecting the drawings. Gratitude is also due to Lisa Brant, Archivist at Stratford, and Professor Margaret Spicer at Dartmouth for their important contributions. As a result of this thoughtful work, we have the opportunity to study a range of examples from some of the outstanding theatre designers at Stratford; and to have a more detailed look at the work of one of these designers, Desmond Heeley, who has been associated with the Festival since 1957.

Both the exhibition and book appropriately focus our attention on the importance of the theatre designer's art. Although there are extensive writings on many aspects of the visual arts (indeed, some of these works properly take their place on a list of the masterpieces of literary art or cultural history), the role of the visual artist in deepening our understanding of the written or spoken word has not been so well recognized among art history scholars. It seems entirely appropriate, therefore, that both the exhibition and book focus our attention on the importance of the theatre designer's art. The challenge facing the theatre designer—often practicing his or her art in collaboration with others, especially the play's director—is to create visual elements that will provide an important imaginative dimension to the staging of a dramatic production. The examples that are shown here clearly express the interpretive vision of the artist. They are more than instructions to costume makers or set designers. Each inspired drawing stands as a work of art. Transcending its classification as theatre memorabilia, each drawing serves, in the words of James Cuno, as "a metaphor for the play itself!"

Parnassus Foundation is honored to be associated with the Hood Museum of Art in encouraging a wider appreciation of the artists whose designs have graced the theatre in Stratford. Their work is testimony to Stratford's continuing commitment to artistic excellence.

Raphael Bernstein
Parnassus Foundation

INTRODUCTION
AND ACKNOWLEDGMENTS

$\mathcal{T}$heatre at Dartmouth has a long tradition, dating back to 1779 when the earliest known American plays, *The Dartmouth Dialogues*, were performed at the College. It has always been a vital part of undergraduate life. The Hopkins Center for the creative and performing arts, which plays host to the Stratford Festival's Fall 1990 Tour and is a partner in the presentation of this exhibition, was conceived in recognition of this fact. Its genesis lay in 1928 when Ernest Martin Hopkins, President of the College, hired Warner Bentley as the College's first Director of Drama, and Churchill P. Lathrop as professor of Art History and soon to be the first Director of the College's Collections and Galleries. Three decades later, under the presidency of John Sloan Dickey, the Hopkins Center was inaugurated as the College's center for the presentation and study of the visual and performing arts. There, in 1980, Arthur Blumenthal, Curator of what was by now called the College's Museum & Galleries, organized *Theater Art of the Medici*, an exhibition which would come to hold a prominent place in the bibliography of theatre history.

We have organized the present exhibition, *Designs for Theatre: Stratford Festival, 1954–1990*, in recognition of Dartmouth's long tradition of excellence in the presentation and study of the visual and performing arts. We also mean to mark the residency of the Stratford Festival at Dartmouth, and to do so by exhibiting thirty-eight of its finest costume designs as preserved in the Festival's Archives. The designs have been selected, it must be said, not for their theatrical value—that is, not for what they tell us about the range of the costumes in Festival productions—but for their value as drawings in their own right. If we had been interested in the former, we might have chosen very different drawings indeed. But we did not. We chose them for their rich and compelling qualities as drawings of the finest kind.

Many people helped to make this exhibition and catalogue possible. First and foremost, Raphael Bernstein, Overseer of the Hopkins Center and the Hood Museum of Art, and member of the Board of Governors of the Stratford Festival, provided much encouragement. In addition, as President of the Parnassus Foundation, he had the idea to mark the Festival's residency at Dartmouth with an exhibition of costume designs from their Archives. The Parnassus Foundation provided guidance throughout the preparation of the exhibition and catalogue, as well as significant financial support throughout the project.

At the Festival, David William, Artistic Director, and Debra Hanson, Head of Design, were supportive of the project from the beginning. Ellen Cole, Director of Communications, was crucial in the early stages, providing us access to the resources of the Festival and hosting our research visit. And Lisa Brant, Archivist, was absolutely essential to its organization. She prepared for our visit, assisted in the selection of the drawings, and provided much needed documentary evidence on the history of the drawings, and we are deeply indebted to her professional commitment to the project. We also acknowledge Desmond Heeley for his many contributions to the catalogue and exhibition.

At the Museum, Margaret Spicer, Adjunct Curator of Costumes and Professor of Drama, not only contributed a most important essay to the catalogue, but helped throughout the preparation of the exhibition. Evelyn Marcus, Curator of Exhibitions, and James Watkinson and Louise Glass of her staff, designed and executed the installation of the exhibition. Kellen Haak, Registrar, and Kimberly King Zea, Assistant Registrar, oversaw the registration of the drawings. Katherine Hart, Curator of Academic Programming, developed curricular programs in conjunction with the exhibition. And Mary McKenna, Elisabeth Gordon, Nancy McLain, and Theresa Delamarre helped in numerous and important ways throughout the project.

At the College, Lynn Britt, Director of the Hopkins Center, and James Steffenson and Lewis Crickard, respectively Professor of Drama and Chair of the Department, provided timely assistance and critical advice, as did Carla Richters, Joan Morris, and Lisa Hodde of the Drama Department Costume Shop.

We thank all of these people for their many contributions. And we acknowledge the continuing support of the Harrington Gallery Fund.

James Cuno
Director, Hood Museum of Art

FOREWORD

$\mathcal{I}$t is universally accepted that the Stratford Festival has been instrumental in altering perceptions about the performance of Shakespeare and other classics in the latter half of the twentieth century. As critic Walter Kerr wrote in 1954, "This theatre is setting a standard for physical production for Shakespearean style, for verse speech, that the rest of this continent can well emulate, and for which it must be very, very deeply grateful."

Despite the inevitable variance in the performance of literally hundreds of plays, in addition to the full canon of Shakespeare, Stratford's production standards have remained consistently high. In designing the thrust stage at Stratford, Tanya Moiseiwitsch and Tyrone Guthrie not only created a model for the world, but established a tradition of excellence which successive artists have disregarded at their peril.

During the last thirty-eight years, designers at Stratford have created enduring stage images. From the "glorious summer" of *Richard III* in 1953 to the autumnal splendour of The Forest of Arden in 1990's *As You Like It*, the design, wardrobe, prop, and scenic departments have been instrumental in bringing the text to life.

The high calibre of artistic material drawn from the Stratford Festival Archives demonstrates the level of achievement of just a few of the notable artists who have been associated with the Festival Theatre. No wonder then that this significant exhibition "Designs for Theatre: Stratford Festival, 1954–1990" inspires one to imagine the day when the Stratford Festival will have its own permanent exhibition space at its home in Stratford, Ontario to share the works of art in our Archives.

The art of design is here accorded not only recognition for its contribution to the creation of the play, but the drawings themselves are appreciated for their intrinsic artistic merit. I applaud the Hood Museum of Art for making this wonderful exhibition possible.

David William
Artistic Director of the Stratford Festival

THOUGHTS ON
THE STRATFORD FESTIVAL

I have special feelings about the Stratford Festival. I went there as a young designer (it seems an age ago now!) and it is a large part of my life.

Through the years it has taught me much about myself, my work, my colleagues, and about friendship.

Its actors too, have taught me much, as have its directors and the many people beyond the theatre's walls, whose lives have mingled with mine.

Stratford has given me the luxury of freedom to pursue my craft in new and different ways, no matter how odd they may have seemed at the time.

It has given everyone who has ever worked there the support and stimulation that comes only when a group of artists work together under one roof.

It has also provided in its workrooms a legendary army of magicians, whose talent, wit, and energy have given form and substance to the sketches and drawings you see in this exhibition from the Festival Archives.

I would like to thank everyone who has made it possible for the drawings to be seen.

Desmond Heeley

Catalogue no. 35

A METAPHOR FOR THE PLAY ITSELF

*A*rtists have long been fascinated with the theater. Some, like Rembrandt, made their studio a stage and dressed their models in costumes and gave them roles as actors in elaborate and fictional historical narratives. Others, like Jacques-Louis David, appropriated the rhetoric of theatrical staging when composing paintings of heroic classical subjects. Still others, like Henri Matisse or Pablo Picasso, or more recently David Hockney, designed for the stage itself, extending into sets, costumes, lighting, and even choreography, the profound beauty of their painted and sculpted art.

Some artists, like those represented here, drew only or primarily for the theatre. They came to see, indeed *drew* to see, their two-dimensional work take life in three dimensions. Just how that happened, how, in the case of costume designers, their drawings were interpreted by the staff in costume workrooms is the subject of Margaret Spicer's essay in this catalogue. I want here to address costume designs as rich and complicated drawings in their own right.

Many of the world's best designers have worked for the Stratford Festival since its founding in 1953. And the Festival's Archives are particularly rich in costume designs. Tanya Moiseiwitsch, for example, Associate Director Laureate of the Festival, first designed for Stratford in its inaugural season, and is represented here by four drawings. The first, a costume design for the Messenger, from *Oedipus Rex* by Sophocles, 1954 (cat. no. 1), is simple and dramatic. It comprises a lone, masked figure drawn in black chalk and opaque washes. With one hand raised and the other outstretched, and with his weight on his back foot, the Messenger rises up as if to bring down thunder from the sky. This emphatic gesture, together with the fearsome expression of his primitive mask, embodies the very violence and archetypal tragedy of the play's drama. As such, the drawing is much more than a set of directions for the craftspeople in the workshop: it is a metaphor for the play itself.

Economy of form and gesture is typical of Moiseiwitsch's bold and dramatic drawing style. One sees it in her costume design for the Queen in Shakespeare's *Cymbeline*, 1970 (cat. no. 8). Here, a figure is rendered alone in a shaft of light, her dress and headdress thickly drawn and fluid, her face caked with thick white gouache, mask-like and expressive of a cold and cunning personality. Evil and villainous, she is alone, one senses, not only because she is a design for one actor's costume, but because she has isolated herself from the world and is a hated subject of others' fears.

The manner of depicting the figure as if she alone embodies the content of the play, is found also in Robert Prévost's design for Mozart's *Don Giovanni*, 1966 (cat. no. 4). Isolated in a field of light, Don Giovanni stands tall. His rich, wine red costume is drawn tight at the waist, accented only by the gold of his belt and the hilt of his sword, and by the white of his collar and cuffs. He is a dashing figure, proud and boastful, vain and deceitful. The sure swipes of the artist's brush define the figure so: the gouache suggesting velvet, the watercolor something more satiny. The vanity of the figure and the richness of his costume, however, leave him vulnerable. Alone in the field of light, he is certain to fall. Indeed, the black cloak draped across his shoulders prefigures his death in the opera's final scene: consumed by the fires of his own selfish passions, Don Giovanni is killed and condemned to hell.

Not all costume designs are as monumental as these, of course, just as not all plays are tragedies. Many designs are picturesque and mean to capture the peculiar and incidental qualities of character. Martha Jamieson's costume design for Sir Hugh Evans from Shakespeare's *The Merry Wives of Windsor*, 1958 (cat. no. 2), for example, is a free and charming indication of the Welsh Parson's fairy scene costume. The quick, impulsive sketching of the figure and the delicate handling of the watercolor give a sprightly quality to the character, just as the long-pointed nose and ass ears make him seem foolish and a bit devilish, a player in a farce for others' amusement. A similar, sure, and quick-wristed rendering is that of Mrs. Peachum by Brian Jackson for a production of *The Beggar's Opera* by John Gay, 1958 (cat. no. 3). Here watercolor washes are used to suggest the full and heavy folds of Mrs. Peachum's somewhat tattered dress. The state of her costume, soiled from having been worn too much, is coincident with the state of her character: she is a petty opportunist, and her sad and overly painted face tells us so.

The conjunction of character and costume is central to costume design. The many-layered and exuberant costume of Fyokla by Murray Laufer for Gogol's *The Marriage Brokers*, 1973 (cat. no. 13), is appropriate to the full-bodied, red-cheeked, and gossipy nature of Fyokla herself. She is a charming and bothersome character, on the margins of society but central to the lives of many. And Laufer's comical drawing style is just right: the simple, bell-shaped silhouette of the figure and the warm and light-filled watercolor renderings of many different fabrics is the image of the village gossip, the shuffling figure who carries news from one person to another, lighting fires all along the way.

This is even more apparent in Debra Hanson's sure and sophisticated design for Court Lady No. 2 for Shakespeare's *As You Like It*, 1990 (cat. no. 21). The exquisitely exaggerated silhouette, rendered in sweeping and delicate purple and brown washes, is as artificial as the Court Lady herself. Her life, as attendant to the court, is as mannered in its protocol and rehearsed patterns of behavior, as her hat is ridiculous, her wig extreme, and her painted face formal and controlled. She is a mannequin: poised and decorative, an ornamental participant in the entertainments of the court.

Other costume designs, while suggesting the personality of the characters for whom they are intended, have a kind of graphic independence, as it were. Susan Benson's design for Fraülein Schneider for *Cabaret*, 1987 (cat. no. 19), and Christina Poddubiuk's design for the Cricket Men of Shakespeare's *The Merry Wives of*

Windsor, 1990 (cat. 20), for example, give a clear sense of their respective characters. Fraülein Schneider is old and world-weary, tired of the complications and complexities of Weimar Berlin. Her frock and "overall" (apron) are simple and simply patterned, drawn with modest means but a sure hand. Her stockings fall heavy at her ankles, and touches of yellow chalk suggest the soiling that discolors them. Her face betrays the burden of time, as pen lines define pinched brows and drawn lips, and white gouache and yellow chalk give substance to her flesh. The Townsmen, on the other hand, are silly and shallow, caricatures of smart and natty gentlemen. Their faces are twisted into doughy grins. Their postures are relaxed but posed. They look less like real people than comic types—Dick Van Dyke, Stan Laurel, or Tweedle-Dee and Tweedle-Dum—buffoons who can sometimes be mean-spirited.

But what's striking about Benson and Poddubiuk's designs is how they were finished off. Unlike those of Moiseiwitsch, Prévost, Jackson, and Hanson, which emphasize the costume and character of a single, isolated figure, these drawings consume the sheets of paper on which they were drawn. The background of The Townsmen, for example, comprises pale green and yellow washes laid down wet to puddle up and leave passages of suspended pigments. To these, on the drawing's right side, yellow wash was splattered for simple graphic effect. It was not meant to suggest stage lighting or articulate further the Townsmen's characters: it was meant simply to complete the drawing as such. This is true also of Benson's design for Fraülein Schneider. The beautiful washes of purple over gray, which define the drawing's field, are not meant to suggest a particular stage set or spatial ambience. They are the field of the drawing itself and, as such, are decorated with splatters of gold wash and the rough-textured, orange chalk script of the artist's hand. Neither the splatters nor the chalk marks contribute to the expression of character in Fraülein Schneider, nor are they necessary for communicating the particulars of her costume: they are drawing marks, pure and simple, ways of completing a drawing, which carry the mood of the play not by what they describe but what they suggest: a pictorial metaphor for the play itself, the tone, rhythm, and character of its content.

This sense of graphic independence is developed further in designs by Mary Kerr, Annena Stubbs, and David Walker. Kerr's design, for the Host of *Candide*, 1978 (cat. no. 16), is a jubilant display of color and pattern. Washes of red, blue, and purple flow up, down, and out to suggest the billowing silk and floppy feathers of an exotic magus. But, even more, they refer to the history of costume itself: to the many 18th-century lampoons of aristocratic dress and coquetry, and the highly ornamental costume designs and drawings of the early 20th-century Russian artists, Alexandre Benois and Leon Bakst. Similarly, however much Annena Stubbs' designs for The Duke of Shakespeare's *Othello* and Burgundy of Shakespeare's *King Lear*, 1972 (cat. nos. 11–12), suggest the fabric-layered costumes for which they were made, they also refer to the experimental graphics of 1960s poster-design and to the highly experimental and controversial costume designs of Stubbs' English colleague, Ralph Koltai.

Such self-consciousness, by which costume designs reflect equally upon their

15

graphic sources as upon the particular demands of the costumes and productions for which they were made, is most apparent in David Walker's design for Capulet for Shakespeare's *Romeo and Juliet*, 1984 (cat. no. 18). Here, although one has a sense of the fabric, silhouette, and detailing of Capulet's costume, one is drawn more to the drawing itself. Its prepared paper suggests antique vellum. Its coloring is like that of a 16th-century illuminated manuscript. And its witty play of illusion, by which one seems to see torn papers pinned together and tacked to a stone wall, suggests a handbill as it might have been on the streets of London outside the Globe Theatre on the eve of the play's original performance. It is a clever and accomplished drawing, suggestive of costume, character, and ambience, and beautiful in its own right. In this respect, in its totality as a drawn sheet of paper, it could not be farther from the costume designs of Moiseiwitsch, Prévost, or Brian Jackson.

The drawings discussed thus far represent the range and quality of costume designs in the Archives of the Stratford Festival, and they, with a few others, comprise the first part of our exhibition. The second part is dedicated to the work and career of a single designer, one whose career dates back almost to the origin of the Festival, and whose work is richly represented in the Festival Archives.

Desmond Heeley began designing for Stratford in 1957, having been brought to the Festival by his mentor, Tanya Moiseiwitsch, with whom he had worked at Stratford-upon-Avon. In all, he has designed twenty-nine productions for the Festival, including *Phaedra*, which was performed at Dartmouth during the Festival's residency at the Hopkins Center.

In many ways, *Phaedra* is typical of Heeley's grand pictorial style. The figure is rendered in profile and made of quick and sure swipes of the brush. There is no underdrawing of graphite, no precise delineation of form, no description of character. There is only layer upon layer of color, passage upon passage of pure paint. Any suggestion of drama lies in the energy of the brushwork itself, in the way it textures the grey charcoal paper and reads like flames dancing in the cold darkness of night.

Indeed, Heeley is a painterly draftsman who builds his characters by metaphor. His Devil Dogs for Shakespeare's *The Tempest*, 1982 (cat. no. 33), are suggestive of marine creatures: "*Not* real doggies," he writes along the bottom of the drawing, "[b]ut a touch of the sea about them—scales. Fins prickly things." They are creatures of the underworld, beasts of the dark unknown, primitive figures who stalked the dark imaginations of Europeans confronted for the first time by the bizarre and exotic tales of new worlds across the sea (cat. no. 34). In these drawings, as in the design for Phaedra, Heeley paints his figures. They are rendered as if transformed or metamorphosed, the result of improvisation. This is true also of Peaseblossom for Shakespeare's *A Midsummer Night's Dream*, 1984 (cat. no. 35). Here the impish, gnome-like figure seems to emerge from the flora in which he sits. His trousers, shirt, and hair appear to sprout naturally from his nut-like head, while his mischievous grin is that of nature herself: a powerful trickster to whom humankind is but a toy.

Heeley's drawing style is perfectly suited to the fantasy world of Shakespeare's comedies. But it is no less capable of rendering the descriptive and ornamental qualities of romantic and historical characters, as in his designs for Ferdinand and Guard/Attendant for *The Duchess of Malfi* by John Webster, 1971 (cat. no. 32). Here the artist's sensitivity to texture is evident in the fine detailing of the figures' trunk-hose, doublets, cloaks, and collars. His control of ink and gouache washes in the articulation of that texture is extraordinary; just as his use of collage emphasizes the shimmering surfaces of the fabrics from which these costumes would be made. Similar effects are achieved by the ink washes that describe the different textures in the costume of a Musketeer from *The Three Musketeers*, designed by Heeley in 1968. Although perhaps less experimental than those for Ferdinand and Guard/Attendant, the rendering of the Musketeer is no less accomplished.

Heeley has said that his Stratford drawings reveal his maturing as a draftsman. Certainly one senses in his design for Sir Walter Blunt for Shakespeare's *Henry IV, Part I*, 1965 (cat. no. 23), a more deliberate hand, one that moves slowly and carefully in the building of form, than in his more recent drawings. Indeed, the blocky and powerful figure of Sir Walter is all silhouette: there are no signs of improvisation, of working the surface with speed and confidence. Three years later, however, in the designs for *The Taming of the Shrew* (cat. nos. 29–31), one sees a whole new artist. A ballpoint pen has moved quickly and freely, rendering the character of each figure, searching for the right gesture and appropriate expression, and building a wiry skeleton to which colored chalks, ink, and gouache and watercolor washes add the details of props and costume. These are wonderful drawings, as playful as they are perceptive, and as uninhibited as they are sure and confident.

I have written of these drawings, Heeley's and the others, as if they were independent works of art. And I believe they can be seen as such. But we must never lose sight of the fact that they were drawn on commission for the purpose of providing someone else with directions for cutting and building a costume. They were, each of them, but one step in the long, many-stepped process of producing a play. Unlike the other steps, however—unlike even the costumes, sets, and props that are kept in theatrical warehouses and used and reused for years—the drawings retain a life of their own. Long after the play is over, the designs remain, and like any other highly accomplished work of graphic art, are to be treasured for their special pictorial beauty. They are, simply put, works of art that stand the test of time in their own right. And this is the point of the exhibition they comprise: they represent a celebration of the art of costume design, an art richly preserved in the Archives of the Stratford Festival.

James Cuno

Catalogue no. 7

BEYOND THE DRAWING:
THE RENDERING INTERPRETED

*T*he challenging and rewarding process of bringing a script to life onstage is the result of a collaborative effort among theatre artists: directors, designers, craftspeople, technicians, stage managers, musicians and actors.

Commencing as much as a year in advance of the production date, the director and designers—costume, scene and lighting—meet for lengthy discussions to discover and establish the overall concept, visual style, and historical period for the production. As they explore the nuances of the script and characters, the social and political background of the play, and the art, architecture, and dress of the given period, the stage director inspires and guides his colleagues toward a mutual interpretation of the play as well as an artistic concept for the production.

Since the primary purpose of costume design is to communicate information to the audience about the characters and the world of the play, it is essential that the director and costume designer thoroughly discuss and agree on character interpretation. Information such as social and economic status, sense of humor, psychological state, and occupation, as well as location, season, time of day, and occasion may be incorporated in the costume. Using the artist's tools of line, texture, and color, the costume designer manipulates the silhouette, garment shapes, materials, and colors of the costume in order to communicate the desired information to the audience.

The costume designer begins putting ideas on paper in the form of rough sketches while continuing conversations with the director. When the costume design crystallizes and the desired results have been achieved, the color renderings are completed and submitted for the director's approval.

As construction commences, the renderings serve as vehicles to communicate the designer's ideas to everyone involved in the production. For the costume designer, these include the director, other designers, and actors, as well as those who will build the costumes and accessories: the cutter/drapers, first hands, stitchers, milliners, wigmakers, armor specialists, jewelers, bootmakers, and painter/dyers.

Generally speaking, the community of artisans responsible for bringing the costume from design to reality share a common aesthetic vision. They understand information in an historical context, as well as the complexities of construction and how various materials respond. No matter how skilled and talented are the artists responsible for implementing the designer's ideas, thorough communication between designer and craftspeople is essential to ensure the success of the completed costume. At the heart of this dialogue is the rendering, the designer's illustration of the costume.

In scene design as in architecture, it is customary for designers to present their ideas in two forms, renderings and models. Scene designers and architects also provide detailed working drawings, ground plans, and elevations drawn to scale, in order to coordinate complex construction and ensure that their ideas will be accurately realized. With costume design it is virtually impossible to provide scale drawings, since one is designing and constructing garments for the infinite variations presented by the human body. Hence the rendering of the costume design must include the essential information, structural and aesthetic, required to build the costume.

Normally, the costume designer is expected to illustrate the costume on the body so that the viewer understands the garments and accessories as well as the personality of the character and the style of the production. There is no question that Shakespeare's *Merry Wives of Windsor* is a comedy, given the humor evident in Christina Poddubiuk's design for the Cricket Men resplendent in 1890s cricket gear (cat. no. 20); or that Shakespeare's *Henry IV, Part I* (cat. no. 23) is a powerfully dramatic history play from the manner in which Desmond Heeley has drawn Sir Walter Blunt, "newly lighted from his horse," confronting the viewer head on with his feet rooted squarely to the ground.

As students, aspiring designers are usually taught to position the figure on the center of the page, opened out in a three-quarter view, with as little distortion or foreshortening as possible. How the designer then arranges the torso, arms, legs, and head greatly assists the cutter/drapers and wardrobe (costume shop) staff in understanding the shape of the garments. Mary Kerr's whimsical Host from *Candide* (cat. no. 16), standing with his arms outstretched, is drawn to reveal the shape of his striped caftan. Had the Host been drawn standing with his arms at the side, the cut and shape of the robe would have been indiscernible.

Occasionally a costume will require that it be illustrated from a side or back view, as in Desmond Heeley's design for the Bishop in *Richard III* (cat. no. 25). However, this arrangement is more commonly seen in explanatory rough sketches which sometimes accompany the finished rendering. Also somewhat unusual are illustrations of multiple characters, characters which function onstage as a chorus or, because of the nature of the plot, are frequently blocked onstage together. Desmond Heeley's striking illustrations of Ferdinand and Guard/Attendant (cat. no. 32) and the Devil Dogs (cat. nos. 33 and 34) provide superb examples of multiple character illustrations.

Frequently a character changes costume during the course of the play. It is customary to render each of the costumes on a separate piece of paper. The exception to this practice may occur when a costume contains several layers which are added or removed onstage, as in Leslie Hurry's design for the great-coat and dress coat and trousers worn by Khlestakov in *The Government Inspector* (cat. no. 7) and Susan Benson's design for the dress and "overall" (apron) worn by Fraülein Schneider in *Cabaret* (cat. no. 19).

The complexity of the costumes as well as the designer's rendering style determine the need for explanatory sketches to assist the construction staff in the workrooms. Clear precise renderings, such as Debra Hanson's design for Court Lady

No. 2 in *As you Like It* (cat. no. 22), rarely require additional sketches. When such sketches are provided, they are usually of the thumbnail variety and added to the margins of the designer's rendering. Three charming and humorous thumbnail sketches surround Martha Jamieson's design for Sir Hugh Evans in *The Merry Wives of Windsor* (cat. no. 2), each explaining the comical placement of orange foxtails on various parts of Evans' anatomy.

Over the years, Desmond Heeley has moved away from drawing precise costume illustrations. Eschewing the detail normally seen in costume renderings, Heeley evokes a powerful sense of characterization, production style, and historical period through the sensuous use of line and the luminous layering of paint, texture, and collage. His recent design for Phaedra (cat. no. 36) is a particularly breathtaking example of this remarkable illustration style.

When one speaks about the evolution of Desmond Heeley's rendering style it is important to note that this style is inextricably linked to Heeley's development of design aesthetics—a series of imaginative and innovative techniques for texturing, layering, and painting fabric surfaces, often the hallmark of a Desmond Heeley production. As a result of the two—the drawing style and the treatment of fabric surfaces—Heeley has become adept at augmenting his color renderings with black and white sketches (beautiful drawings in and of themselves) illustrated with copious instructions rich in visual imagery, explaining how the costume is to be constructed, textured, and painted. On the sketch for Theramenes in *Phaedra* (cat. no. 38), Desmond Heeley explains how the fabric is to be handled: "Scraps of black wool cut on the bias & machined to a thin fabric—washing machined—(to look like a ploughed field) & applied to the *highlight* of the garment. Green grey scrap wool on *inside* stripe for outer drape (this to come & go in movement)."

For the Devil Dogs (cat. no. 33) Heeley describes the effect desired of the surface textures: "Mysterious surface & textures. *Not* real doggies—But a touch of the sea about them—scales. Fins prickly things—Could have a wet kind of glitter. Paws." Informative yet poetic instructions like these capture the imagination of the reader as well as instruct the craftspeople responsible for their implementation.

Before construction can begin on the costumes, the costume designer and wardrobe supervisor purchase fabrics and trimmings. Selecting fabrics for use in the theatre is only a start. Frequently materials are dyed in yardage or painted and overdyed once the costume is completed. A rendering may assist and direct this process by indicating how the fabric subsequently will be treated by the painter/dyer. For *King Lear* and *Othello* (cat. nos. 11 and 12) Annena Stubbs sponged, stenciled, and sprayed the paint onto her renderings. This illustration technique suggests that Stubbs intended that the fabric yardage and finished costumes be treated in a similar manner, since the fabric rendered would not have been commercially available by the yard. Likewise, the splatter technique used by David Walker on his design for Capulet in *Romeo and Juliet* (cat. no. 18) suggests that a similar painting technique was desired on the finished costume in order to mottle the fabric surface under light, recreating the richness of Italian Renaissance velvet.

When the costume designer and wardrobe staff commence discussions about how the designs will be constructed and realized, they must examine the many components which constitute a costume. Typically they begin with the body shape required for the character, then work through each garment layer: corset, petticoats, gown, shawl, etc., as well as the accessories worn or carried, plus the hat, wig, and makeup.

In a repertory theatre company such as the Stratford Festival, an actor may play several roles throughout a season of plays, often returning for successive seasons. It becomes especially important that the actor be virtually transformed for each role, that the costume assist the creation of a unique character for each production. Body padding is a very effective means of achieving this end, adding physical age and weight to the performer. The padding may be subtle, creating minor changes in the actor's natural body proportion, or appropriately exaggerated to suit the character and style of the production, as in Desmond Heeley's design for the cheerful Hostess in *Henry V* (cat. no. 24).

Just as padding can alter the physical aspect of the actor, so wigs and facial hair can dramatically transform the actor's appearance, expressing characterization and historical period. Due to the scale of a costume rendering, it is usually impossible to provide enough visual detail to inform the hair department about the size, cut, and styling of a wig or facial hair. Tanya Moiseiwitsch's sketches for Belarius and Caius Lucius in *Cymbeline* (cat. nos. 9 and 10) are handsome examples of the type of drawings required.

Makeup is also an important tool for the costume designer and actor in their combined effort to define a character. In the theatre, in contrast to film and television, actors often create and apply their own makeup. The designer's rendering may be used to inspire a basic concept for a makeup design. For instance, Desmond Heeley's humorous illustration of the drunken Christopher Sly (cat. no. 30), standing in profile, tankard in hand, with his head thrown back and his bulbous nose pointing to the sky, could be used as the basis for the creation of a prosthetic nose piece. On the other hand, Murray Laufer's drawing of the rosy, round-cheeked, smiling Fyokla from *The Marriage Brokers* (cat. no. 13), is a makeup design in and of itself. Given the rotund figure of the character, devising the optical illusion of a very round face to balance the actress' padded body would be essential to the success of the overall costume.

Occasionally face masks are used in lieu of makeup, most often for productions of the ancient Greek and Roman comedies and tragedies. Utilizing stylized facial expressions, masks are a powerful means of expressing character. Tanya Moiseiwitsch's costume and mask design for the Messenger in Sir Tyrone Guthrie's legendary 1954 production of *Oedipus Rex* (cat. no. 1) is a noteworthy example.

It is customary for the design team to present their drawings and models to the cast at the first read-through of the play. If the director and the designer have been successful in their collaboration, the image of the costume will support and enhance the powers of the actor throughout the rehearsal process as he makes choices about his walk, gestures, and character qualities. A particularly effective example of how costume can inform the performer is seen in Leslie Hurry's design for Khlestakov, the imposter inspector general in *The Government Inspector* (cat. no. 7). By illustrating Khlestakov in profile with puffed-up chest, head tilted back in a snooty leer (Hurry describes him as "faded—down at heel—dusty"), the designer has managed to convey the correct pose of an early nineteenth-century dandy, as well as create a body carriage with which the actor can experiment. Equally useful are the stance and facial expression in Brian Jackson's design for the haughty Mrs. Peachum in *The Beggar's Opera* (cat. no. 3).

On a practical level, the costume designer's rendering can be used to educate the actor in the correct way to stand and sit in a period costume, also how to handle such awkward accessories as swords, capes, hats, and fans. It is usually the costume designer's responsibility to explain the subtleties of period movement and to coach the actor in the correct way to move in the costume. This process commences in the costume fittings when all the components of the design come together and the costume begins to take shape.

Careful study of historical source material, such as portraits and photographs, can teach one much about how to move in the clothes of a given period. Often designers carry this information into their costume renderings. Two superb examples are Desmond Heeley's design for a Musketeer in *The Three Musketeers* (cat. no. 26) and Robin Fraser Paye's rendering of Margaret and Ursula in *Much Ado About Nothing* (cat. no. 17).

Standing with his left hand on his hip holding back the folds of the cape and with his right leg turned out, Heeley's Musketeer is the epitome of the cavalier gentleman seen in the Van Dyck portraits of the 1620s and 1630s. Since the wide cuffs on a pair of seventeenth-century boots prevent an actor from bringing his legs close together, it is more comfortable to stand with one foot away from the body and with the hand positioned on the opposite hip for balance, or on the hilt of the sword as in Robert Prévost's design for Don Giovanni (cat. no. 4). Balanced by the heels on the boots, the weight of the cape and large hat, the costume eases the body quite naturally into the pose and swaggering walk of a seventeenth-century cavalier.

Robin Fraser Paye's exquisite illustration for Margaret and Ursula (cat. no. 17) is another excellent example of period posture and movement incorporated into the designer's rendering. The corset of the 1620s and 1630s requires one to sit with a straight torso and assists the wearer in holding her head high. Both enhance the line of the neck which is emphasized by the hairstyle and horizontal neckline of the period. Note the elegant line created by Margaret's fan as it extends the length of her arm; also, the graceful way Ursula gathers her voluminous skirts to the side as she sits forward in the chair in a correct pose for the period. Robin Fraser Paye has thoughtfully and eloquently incorporated images and information into this rendering, undoubtedly assisting the actresses as they prepared to move in the costumes as if they had lived in these clothes all their lives.

During the process of realizing the designer's ideas onstage, many purposes are served by the costume designer's rendering. Though often handsome and stunning drawings, they are but a means to an end, coming alive and assuming meaning only when the resulting costumes are worn by actors and seen by an audience in the context of a specifically conceived and designed production. Only then do the renderings and costumes communicate the information they were designed to impart, and fullfill their function in the art of the theatre.

Margaret E. Spicer

CATALOGUE OF THE EXHIBITION

PART I
STRATFORD FESTIVAL DESIGNS

1 Tanya Moiseiwitsch

*Costume design for the Messenger, for the production of
"Oedipus Rex" by Sophocles,* 1954

Pen and ink, black chalk, with watercolor washes on
prepared paper
15 x 12 in.
The Messenger was performed by Douglas Rain

Tanya Moiseiwitsch, Associate Director Laureate of
the Stratford Festival, first designed for Stratford in its
inaugural season in 1953. Having come to Stratford
from London's Old Vic Theatre, with Sir Tyrone
Guthrie, the Festival's first artistic director, Tanya
Moiseiwitsch has designed many productions and, with
Sir Tyrone, Stratford's original thrust stage. In addition, she collaborated with the architect Robert Fair-
field on the design of the permanent theater itself. Her
celebrated career has included designing for Stratford-
upon-Avon's Shakespeare Memorial Theatre, the National Theatre of Great Britain, the Old Vic, Dublin's
Abbey Theatre, the Guthrie Theatre, where she was
named principal designer in 1963, the Metropolitan
Opera, and the Royal Opera at Covent Garden.

MESSENGER

2 MARTHA JAMIESON

Costume design for Sir Hugh Evans, for the production of Shakespeare's "The Merry Wives of Windsor," 1956

Graphite, red chalk, and watercolor and ink washes on wove paper
13^{17}/$_{18}$ x 6⅜ in.
Sir Hugh Evans was performed by Eric House

ERIC HOUSE
"EVANS"

Jamieson /56

3 BRIAN JACKSON

*Costume design for Mrs. Peachum, for the production
of "The Beggar's Opera" by John Gay, 1958*

Pen and ink with watercolor washes on wove paper
13½ x 9¹⁷⁄₁₈ in.
Mrs. Peachum was performed by Ann Casson

Originally from England, Brian Jackson came to Canada in 1955 to head the properties department of the Stratford Festival, a position he held until 1963. In 1962 he collaborated with Tanya Moiseiwitsch on the remodelling of the Festival Theatre thrust stage. Among his list of twenty-five design credits for the Festival include *The Two Gentlemen of Verona*, *H.M.S. Pinafore*, *The Rise and Fall of the City of Mahagonny*, *The Cherry Orchard*, *Twelfth Night*, and *Waiting for Godot*. Mr. Jackson has designed for most of Canada's leading theatres, including the Shaw Festival, the Canadian Opera Company, the National Arts Centre, and the Vancouver Playhouse.

Mrs Peachum

BRIAN JACKSON.
1958.

4 ROBERT PRÉVOST

Costume design for Don Giovanni, for the production
of the opera of the same title by W. A. Mozart, 1966
Pen and ink with gouache on cardboard
14¾ x 10½ in.
Don Giovanni was performed by Cornelis Opthof

Now deceased, Robert Prévost first began designing as
a student with the Holy Cross Fathers in Montreal. He
designed for Les Compagnons de Saint-Laurent, the
Montreal Festivals Society, the Toronto Opera Festival,
Le Théâtre du Nouveau Monde in Montreal, and the
Canadian Broadcasting Company. He is considered
among the finest native Canadian designers.

Don Giovanni

Don Giovanni, Act I, Scene II

Prévost

5 LESLIE HURRY

Set design for the production of "The Government In-
spector" by Nikolai Gogol, as adapted by Peter Raby,
1967
Pen and ink, with graphite, gouache, watercolor, and
charcoal on wove paper
8 x 11¼ in.

Now deceased, Leslie Hurry was born in England and
studied at St. John's Wood Art School and London's
Royal Academy. Following a twelve-year period in
which he travelled throughout Great Britain and lived
in Paris painting and exhibiting surrealist-inspired
landscape pictures, Mr. Hurry turned to designing for
the theatre. His first designs were for the Sadler's Wells
Ballet production of *Hamlet* in 1943. Eight years later
he designed *Tamburlaine the Great* by Christopher Mar-
lowe for Sir Tyrone Guthrie at the Old Vic. When
Guthrie directed a second *Tamburlaine* for the Stratford
Festival company in 1956, Mr. Hurry was its designer.
Although he would not return to Canada until 1964,
Mr. Hurry came to work there almost exclusively. His
designs for the Stratford Festival included *King Lear*,
Julius Caesar, *A Midsummer Night's Dream*, *The School
for Scandal*, and *Pericles*.

6 LESLIE HURRY

Set design for the production of "The Government Inspector" by Nikolai Gogol, as adapted by Peter Raby, 1967

Pen and ink, with graphite, gouache, watercolor, and charcoal on wove paper
8 x 11¼ in.

7 LESLIE HURRY

Costume design for Khlestakov, for the production of
"The Government Inspector" by Nikolai Gogol, as
adapted by Peter Raby, 1967

Pen and ink, with graphite and chalk on wove paper
15 x 11⅜ in.
Khlestakov was performed by William Hutt

Klestakov — faded — down at heel — dusty

8 Tanya Moiseiwitsch

*Costume design for the Queen, for the production of
Shakespeare's "Cymbeline,"* 1970

Graphite, pen and ink, with watercolor and gouache
washes with collage on wove paper
17 x 10½ in.
The Queen was performed by Pat Galloway

The QUEEN   CYMBELINE

T.M.
'70

9 TANYA MOISEIWITSCH

*Wig and beard design for Belarius, for the production
of Shakespeare's "Cymbeline,"* 1970

Graphite and watercolor wash on wove paper
8½ x 11 in.
Belarius was performed by Mervyn Blake

Mr MERVYN BLAKE   CYMBELINE
BELARIUS

Uneven
line of
curls on
brow, and long
at nape.

Crisp grey flecked with white
curls, close to the head.

Curly grey/white beard & moustache.

10 TANYA MOISEIWITSCH

Wig and beard design for Caius Lucius, for the production of Shakespeare's "Cymbeline," 1970

Graphite and watercolor wash on wove paper
8½ x 11 in.
Caius Lucius was performed by James Blendick

MR J BLENDICK   CYMBELINE
CAIUS LUCIUS

Grey stubbly curls, Renaissance
style, Roman ambassador/general
in the Army.   No parting.
Tight curly beard, slightly darker grey.

11 ANNENA STUBBS

*Costume design for Burgundy, for the production of
Shakespeare's "King Lear," 1972*

Pen and ink with colored ink stamping on wove paper
22 x 14¾ in.
Burgundy was performed by Don Sutherland

Born in England, Annena Stubbs studied at London's
Central School of Arts and Crafts. Ms. Stubbs launched
her career in the field of opera design, and has frequently designed for Sadler's Wells operatic productions. She first designed for the Stratford Festival in
1971, for its production of *Volpone* by Ben Jonson. She
has also designed for the Royal Shakespeare Company
and the National Theatre of Great Britain.

Burgundy.

King Lear.   Armena Stull 72

12 ANNENA STUBBS

Costume design for the Duke, for the production of Shakespeare's "Othello," 1973

Pen and ink with colored ink stamping and metallic spray paint on wove paper
21¾ x 14¾ in.
The Duke was performed by William Needles

Duke.

Othello - Duke
Armena Stacks. 78

13 MURRAY LAUFER

Costume design for Fyokla, for the production of "The Marriage Brokers" by Nikolai Gogol, 1973

Graphite, pen and ink, with watercolor and gouache washes on wove paper, and fabric swatches
15^{17}/$_{18}$ x 11^{17}/$_{18}$ in.
Fyokla was performed by Lila Kaye

Born in Toronto, Murray Laufer studied at the Ontario College of Art. He first worked for the Canadian Broadcasting Corporation, designing various television productions, from drama to musical variety shows. Then, in the mid-1950s, he began designing for theatre and opera. Since then, Mr. Laufer has designed numerous productions for the Canadian Opera Company, the Crest Theatre, the National Arts Centre of Ottawa, and the St. Lawrence Centre. He first worked for the Stratford Festival in 1973, designing the much acclaimed *The Marriage Brokers*.

Fyohla
Miss Kaye

FLASHY COMB
IN BUN AT BACK
EAR, RINGS.

RINGS
BRACLETS

BLACK THICK
SOCKS

14 STRATFORD FESTIVAL DESIGN TEAM

*Costume design for Amanda, for the production of
"Private Lives" by Noel Coward*, 1978

Graphite and colored pencil with watercolor on wove
paper
14⅞ x 10½ in.
Amanda was performed by Maggie Smith

Rarely were designs for Stratford Festival productions
executed or conceived by more than one individual. In
this instance, the team of designers included Daphne
Dare, Michael Maher, and John Pennoyer. All drawings
were left unsigned. Daphne Dare first worked for the
Stratford Festival in 1975, becoming its Head of Design
in 1978. Ms. Dare has worked extensively at Stratford,
as well as in London's West End, Los Angeles, and for
BBC Television. Michael Maher first worked for Stratford in 1978, after winning the Canadian Opera Company's Young Designer Competition in 1976. Well-
known for his innovative design sketches, Mr. Pennoyer
only began working full-time for Stratford in 1980. He
joined the Design Team for this production, however,
after having won the Tom Patterson Award for skill and
commitment in a young designer's work at Stratford.

15 STRATFORD FESTIVAL DESIGN TEAM

Wig Design for Amanda, for the production of "Private Lives" by Noel Coward, 1978

Graphite with collage on wove paper
13¹⁵/18 x 10 in.
Amanda was performed by Maggie Smith

MISS MAGGIE SMITH
AMANDA.
PRIVATE LIVES
AVON THEATRE
STRATFORD ONT '78

16 MARY KERR

Costume design for the Host, for the production of
"Candide" by Voltaire, 1978

Graphite with watercolor washes on wove paper
17¾ x 14¾ in.
The Host was performed by Elias Zarou

Born in Winnipeg, Manitoba, Mary Kerr received her
B.F.A. in Fine Arts at the University of Manitoba, where
she specialized in sculpture. Quickly, however, she
began designing for theatre, and during the past fifteen
years has worked for the Stratford Festival, the Canadian Broadcasting Company, the Canadian Stage Company, and the Canadian Opera Company.

MARY KERR 78   'CANDICE' THE HOST   MR ELIAS ZARDU   STRATFORD 78

17 ROBIN FRASER PAYE

Costume design for Margaret and Ursula, for the pro-
duction of Shakespeare's "Much Ado About Nothing,"
1980

Graphite, pen and ink, chalks, with watercolor washes
on wove paper
23 x 19½ in.
Margaret was performed by Donna Goodhand, and
Ursula by Alicia Jeffery

Born in England, Robin Fraser Paye's first theatrical
engagement was in 1965 when he designed costumes
for the Dublin Festival. The following year he became
Costume Supervisor for the English Stage Company
at the Royal Court Theatre in London. Since then, Mr.
Paye has worked extensively for BBC Television, becoming its Senior Costume Designer in 1980.

"MUCH ADO ABOUT NOTHING"

"Formal Evening Coat for Margaret & Ursula ACT I S3

18 DAVID WALKER

*Costume designs for Capulet, for the production of
Shakespeare's "Romeo and Juliet," 1984*

Pen and ink with watercolor and gouache washes on
prepared paper
19¼ x 13⅝ in.
Capulet was performed by Kenneth Pogue

British born, David Walker has worked in theatre for
more than thirty years, designing sets and costumes
for the National Theatre of Great Britain, the Royal
Shakespeare Company, the English National Opera,
the Metropolitan Opera, Covent Garden, Sadler's
Wells, and the Stratford Festival.

Romeo and Juliet

Ye Capulet

Shakespeare's in Tudors

Stratford Ontario

David Walker

1984

19 SUSAN BENSON

Costume design for Fraülein Schneider, for the production of "Cabaret," book by Joe Masteroff, based on a play by John Van Druten and stories by Christopher Isherwood, 1987

Graphite, pen and ink, with watercolor and gouache washes on wove paper, with fabric swatches
22⅞ x 14½ in.
Fraülein Schneider was performed by Denise Ferguson

Trained in England, Susan Benson moved to Canada in 1966, where she first worked as assistant costume designer for the Queen Elizabeth Playhouse of Vancouver. Her Stratford Festival productions include *Twelfth Night*, *The Taming of the Shrew*, *The Mikado*, and *Macbeth*. The winner of six Dora Mavor Moore Awards for design excellence, Ms. Benson has twice represented Canada at the Prague Quadrennials, and has designed for ballet and opera companies throughout North America.

20 CHRISTINA PODDUBIUK

Costume designs for the Cricket Men, for the production of Shakespeare's "The Merry Wives of Windsor,"
1990

Graphite, pen and ink, with watercolor washes on wove paper, with fabric swatches
14¼ x 10⅞ in.

Canadian born, Christina Poddubiuk was educated at McGill University and the National Theatre School in Montreal. She has worked throughout Canada, and has designed for the Stratford Festival since 1982.

Cricket Men
The Merry Wives
of Windsor
Stratford 1990

C. Poddubiuk

21 DEBRA HANSON

Costume design for Apparition King No. 2, from the production of Shakespeare's "Macbeth," 1990

Graphite and ink on wove paper, with fabric swatches
21⅛ x 14⅞ in.
Apparition King No. 2 was performed by James Binkley

In her first year as Head of Design for the Stratford Festival, Debra Hanson is the designer of the 1990 productions, *Macbeth*, *As You Like It*, and *The Lunatic, the Lover & the Poet*, the last of which was presented at Dartmouth as part of the Festival's Fall 1990 tour. Ms. Hanson studied at Dalhousie University and the National Theatre School, and has worked with numerous companies across Canada, including the Shaw Festival, CentreStage, Toronto Free Theatre, and the Banff Centre for the Arts. In addition, she has served as Resident Designer for both Theatre New Brunswick and the Manitoba Theatre Centre, and has taught design at Bishop's University, McGill University, and John Abbott College. During her nine seasons at the Stratford Festival, Ms. Hanson has received much acclaim, including the Pauline McGibbon Award in 1984 and a Dora Mavor Moore Award in 1983.

Macbeth   HANSON/90
                    THE STRATFORD FESTIVAL
Apparition King #2   Mr. James Blendick

22 DEBRA HANSON

Costume design for Court Lady No. 2, for the production of Shakespeare's "As You Like It," 1990

Graphite with watercolor and gouache washes on wove paper
16 x 11 in.
Court Lady No. 2 was performed by Janice Luey

THE STRATFORD FESTIVAL
ACT 1 SC 1

MISS PRISM LADY

Court Lady #
B.You Like It

LAWSON/90

PART II

DESMOND HEELEY DESIGNS

*D*esmond Heeley has designed twenty-nine productions for the Stratford Festival, beginning with Shakespeare's *Hamlet* in 1957, which marked the opening of the permanent Festival Theatre at Stratford. His list of Stratford credits includes *The Merchant of Venice* (1989), *The Tempest* and *Arms and The Man* (1982), *Coriolanus* (1981), *The Duchess of Malfi* (1971), and *Cosi Fan Tutte* (1967), many of which are represented by costume designs included here.

As Peter Brook's assistant at the Shakespeare Memorial Theatre, Heeley designed the costumes and properties for the now legendary production of *Titus Andronicus*, with Sir Laurence Olivier and Vivien Leigh. In 1967, he designed the premier production of Tom Stoppard's *Rosencrantz and Guildenstern are Dead* for Great Britain's National Theatre, which won him two Tony Awards on its transfer to Broadway the following year.

In addition to the theatre, Desmond Heeley has designed numerous operatic productions and ballets. These include *Norma* with Joan Sutherland for the Metropolitan Opera, *Faust* with Kiri Te Kanawa for the Royal Opera, Covent Garden, *The Merry Widow* as directed for the Australian Ballet by Sir Robert Helpmann and performed by Dame Margot Fonteyn, and *La Sylphide* for Erik Bruhn and Mikhail Baryshnikov for the American Ballet Theater.

Mr. Heeley's most recent work for the Stratford Festival, *Phaedra*, was presented at Dartmouth as part of the Festival's Fall 1990 tour.

23 DESMOND HEELEY

Costume design for Sir Walter Blunt, for the production of Shakespeare's "Henry IV, Part I," 1965

Graphite, pen and ink, with watercolor washes on wove paper
10 x 14¾ in.
Sir Walter Blunt was performed by Claude Bede

SIR WALTER BLUNT. ACT I SC I   HENRY IV PART I

CLAUDE BEDE.

GREY BLUE WOOL CLOAK,
FINE BROWN WOOL
TUNIC,
TO LOOK VERY SLEEK.

"He's lighted from his
horse"

LINED ON BACK
OT CLOAK .

RIDING BOOTS.

24 DESMOND HEELEY

Costume design for the Hostess, for the production of
Shakespeare's "Henry V," 1966

Graphite, pen and ink, with watercolor washes on wove
paper
13 x 8 in.

HENRY V

HOSTESS

QUILTED COTTON
CARDY.
+ TIE ON SLEEVE
ALL TO HELP
THE WADGE

FABRIC FOR
MAIN COSTUME
MADE FROM
SEWING STRIPS
TOGETHER, LIKE
AN OLD PATCH
WORK QUILT,
ROUGH SIDE
OUT, OLD
SCRAPS
USED

TEXTURE

DH '66

25 DESMOND HEELEY

Costume design for the Bishop, for the production of
Shakespeare's "Richard III," 1967

Graphite, pen and ink, with watercolor washes and collage on wove paper
13⅞ x 8½ in.

RICHARD III   BISHOP.

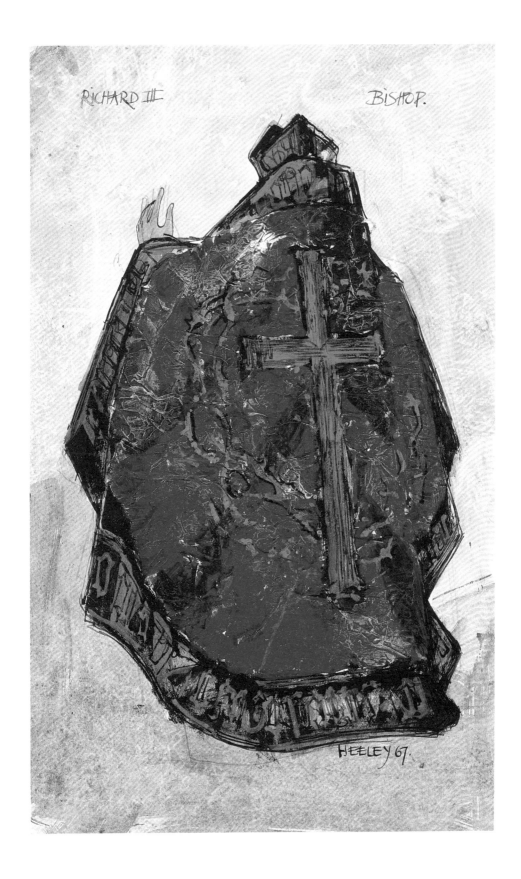

HEELEY 67.

26 DESMOND HEELEY

Costume design for a Musketeer, for the production of
"The Three Musketeers" by Alexandre Dumas,
adapted by Peter Raby, 1968

Graphite, pen and ink, with watercolor and goauche
washes on wove paper
13¾ x 8 in.

HEELEY 68

27 DESMOND HEELEY

Wig, mustache, and goatee design for Aramis, for the production of "The Three Musketeers" by Alexandre Dumas, adapted by Peter Raby, 1968

Graphite, pen, and ink washes on wove paper
10⅞ x 8¾ in.
Aramis was performed by Christopher Newton

3 MUSKETEERS.   STRATFORD.

ARAMIS   CHRISTOPHER NEWTON.

ORSINO WIG.   12ᵗ NIGHT?
NEW BEARD + MOUSTACHE

2. beard & moustache only HEELEY 68

28 DESMOND HEELEY

Moustache design for the 1st English Lord, for the production of "The Three Musketeers" by Alexandre Dumas, adapted by Peter Raby, 1968

Graphite, pen, and ink washes on wove paper
10⅞ x 8⅜ in.
The 1st English Lord was performed by David Foster

3 M'S.

1ST ENGLISH LORD
DAVID FOSTER.

MOUSTACHE ONLY - LARGE, & R·A·F· ISH

MOUSE

VERY FAST CHANGE.   HEELEY '68

29 DESMOND HEELEY

Costume design for Lucentio, for the production of Shakespeare's "The Taming of the Shrew," 1968

Graphite, black chalk, with ink and watercolor washes on wove paper
11 x 8¼ in.
Lucentio was performed by Richard Monette

30 DESMOND HEELEY

Costume design for Christopher Sly, for the production of Shakespeare's "The Taming of the Shrew," 1973

Ballpoint pen, colored chalks, with ink, gouache, and watercolor washes on wove paper
10⅞ x 8½ in.
The part of Christopher Sly was cut from the production and thus, though designed, was not cast

31 DESMOND HEELEY

Costume design for the Pedant, for the production of
Shakespeare's "The Taming of the Shrew," 1973

Ballpoint pen, colored chalks, with ink, gouache, and
watercolor washes on wove paper
10⅞ x 8½ in.
The Pedant was performed by Richard Curnock

TAMING OF THE SHREW   PEDANT.

PACK

32 DESMOND HEELEY

Costume designs for Ferdinand and Guard/Attendant, for the production of "The Duchess of Malfi" by John Webster, 1971

Graphite, pen and ink, with ink and gouache washes
and collage on wove paper
17 x 13½ in.
Ferdinand was performed by Roland Hewgill

THE DUCHESS OF MALFI   FERDINAND GUARD/ATTENDANT.

HEAVY APPLIQUE
BROWN ALMOST
BLACK GOLD—

DOUBLET.
THE TRUNK
HOSE ON
THE PANTS.

BOOTS.

½ CIRCLE
CLOAKS.

SWORD &
SWORD BELT.

NO BUTTONS.
OR FASTENINGS TO SHOW.
FOAM FOR CLOAK — SO
THAT THEY ARE NOT
HEAVY.

HEELEY 71

33 DESMOND HEELEY

Costume designs for the Devil Dogs, for the production of Shakespeare's "The Tempest," 1982

Graphite, pen and ink, with gouache and watercolor washes on wove paper
11 x 12¼ in.

THE TEMPEST   STRATFORD   ONTARIO

BEELER. 82

IF THE DOGS ARE TO CHASE — AN ACTOR FOR EACH ONE
MYSTERIOUS SURPRISE + TEXTURES — NOT REAL DOGGIES —
BUT A TOUCH OF THE SEA ABOUT THEM, — SCALES. FINS
PRICKLY THINGS — COULD HAVE A WET KIND OF GLITTER.
FINS — TO JOIN THE 3 HEADED DOGS —

34 DESMOND HEELEY

Costume designs for the Devil Dogs, for the production of Shakespeare's "The Tempest," 1982

Graphite, pen and ink, with gouache and watercolor washes on wove paper
14 x 11 in.

35 DESMOND HEELEY

Costume design for Peaseblossom, for the production of
Shakespeare's "A Midsummer's Night Dream," 1984

Graphite, acrylic, with gouache and watercolor washes
on wove paper
14½ x 11½ in.
Peaseblossom was performed by Toni LoRaso

PEASEBLOSSOM.

KEELEY 87

A MIDSUMMER NIGHT'S DREAM   STRATFORD ONTARIO

36 DESMOND HEELEY

*Costume design for Phaedra, for the production of
Racine's "Phaedra,"* 1990

Watercolor and gouache on dark, sand-colored wove
paper
$12\frac{7}{8}$ x $19\frac{5}{8}$ in.
Phaedra was performed by Patricia Conolly

37 DESMOND HEELEY

Working sketch for Panope, for the production of
Racine's "Phaedra," 1990

Colored ink and felt-tip pens on wove paper
16½ x 11 in.
Panope was performed by Mary Blendick

`PHAEDRA`   PONORE   MARY BLENDICK.

BLOCK ON BLOCK

BROWN PAPER TAPE BASE
FOR HEADRESS —
PLASTIC NUTS.
SPLIT IN HALF
BRAIDED
ORGANZA FOR
OUTER ROLL
OF HEADDRESS.

OWN HAIR SLICKED
BACK. THE 'NUTS'
WIRED TO PROTRUDE
FORWARD

COLLAR, BELT
& SASH, $\underline{\underline{V}}$
FIRM.
APPLIED POINTED
PLASTIC LEAVES
BEADS ETC.
X THE GLUE
GUN USED
LIKE A POINT
BRUSH. (NOT
BLOBS!)

PLASTIC
(JERSEY)
STICHED
WITH BLACK
RAT TAIL
RIDGES
QUITE
CLOSE
TOGETHER
TO
FORM A
RIPPLE
WHEN
RELEASED

OVER ALL A
MISTING OF
OLIVE SHOE
SPRAY TO
TAKE AWAY
THE CURSE OF
THE BLACK
CRÊPE FABRIC
LOOKING PURPLE
UNDER BLUE
LIGHT

BARE FOOT.

D.H. 90

38 DESMOND HEELEY

Working sketch for Theramenes, for the production of Racine's "Phaedra," 1990

Colored ink and felt-tip pens on wove paper
16½ x 11 in.
Theramenes was performed by Douglas Rain

PHAEDRA   THERAMENES   D. RAIN

(OWN HAIR)

BED BLACK
JERSEY —
LINED. INNER GARMENT
DONGLAS OVERLAID TO
WOOL! —

SLEEVES
LINED.

* SCRAPS OF
BLACK WOOL
CUT ON BIAS &
MACHINED TO A
THIN FABRIC —
WASHING MACH.—
INED — ((TO
LOOK LIKE
PLOUGHED
FIELD)) &
APPLIED TO
THE HIGHLIGHT
OF THE GARMENT

BRAIDED
EDGE →
&
"PLOUGHED
FIELD"
STUFF
ADDED.
TO MAKE
A
FIRM
EDGE.

* GREEN GREY
SCRAP WOOL FOR
INSIDE STRIPE,
FOR OUTER DRAPE
(THIS TO CONVEY
& IN MOVEMENT

x BLACK SOCKS
& SANDALS —
· LOSE THE FEET.

OUTER CLEAR OFF THE GROUND

DESIGNS FOR THEATRE:
STRATFORD FESTIVAL, 1954–1990

has been typeset, printed, and bound by
Meriden-Stinehour Press. The text type is Janson with
Legend for display. The papers used are Monadnock Dulcet
text, Carolina coated cover, and Rainbow Antique endleaves.
An edition of three thousand copies was produced
in October 1990 in Lunenburg, Vermont.
Design by Christopher Kuntze